WHAT DO THEY SAY?

Written by Ruth McNaughton Hinds
Illustrated by Faith McNaughton Lowell

A Tiny Question Book

Port Town Publishing, Superior, WI 54880

Copyright 2004 Lyle and Amy Poster. All rights reserved. Made in the USA. No part of this book may be reproduced or copied in any form without written permission from the copyright owners.
ISBN # 1-59466-051-4

Previously published as 0-88207-062-2

www.bigwoodsbooks.com

"Moo, moo!" says the cow,
"God gives me milk for you."

"Bow wow!" barks the dog,
"God gives me bones to chew."

"Buzz, buzz!" says the bee,
"God helps me make honey."

"Chirp, chirp!" sings the birdie,
"God makes the day sunny."

"Chat, chat!" says the squirrel,
"God gives me soft fur."

"Meow, meow!" says the kitty,
"God helps me to purr."

"Oink, oink!" grunts the pig,
"God makes corn to eat."

"Quack, quack!" says the duck,
"God made my funny feet."

"Baa, baa!" says the sheep,
"God gives me wool for you."

"Gobble, gobble!" calls the turkey,
"God makes feathers too."

"Neigh, neigh!" says the horse,
"God gave me strong legs."

"Cluck, cluck!" says the hen,
"God helps me lay eggs."

"Cock-a-doo!" crows the rooster,
"A good morning God sends."

"Thank You, God," says the child,
"For my bird and animal friends."

14

About the Author

Ruth McNaughton Hinds is a wonderful blessing from the Lord. Ruth is a graduate of Platteville State Teachers' College, in Wisconsin, the Missionary Training Institute at Nyack, New York, and of Wheaton College. Her varied experience includes teaching in rural schools, summer Bible Schools, Sunday Schools and a Papago Indian Mission School in Arizona. Ruth is now 88 years old and an absolute delight to talk with. She loves children and the Lord Jesus very much as her books will surely show.

Amy M. Poster

The Port Town Publishing
Tiny Question Books
is a wonderful collection written
by Ruth McNaughton Hinds.
This series of books is for
nursery-age children, giving
them a solid, basic conception of
God's love, His creation, and
conduct that pleases God. These
are conveyed to impressionable
2's and 3's by colorful pictures
and two or three lines of
rhyming copy

ISBN 1-59466-051-4

$7.95